By Bus

Erica Van Horn

Ugly Duckling Presse
Brooklyn, NY
2021

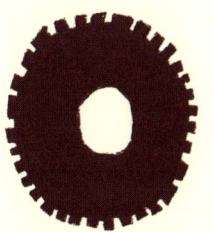

SHARING A SEAT

The woman on the bus spoke in a loud and constant ramble to the man next to her. Her sentences had no full stops and she never paused for a breath. No one sitting nearby could fail to hear her. The man in the seat beside her never said one word. The woman said that her grandmother had taught her how to Tell The Weather and she reckoned it would be dry tomorrow even though the man on her radio had promised rain. She announced, "I do not care if it rains because I am going to be at home all day tomorrow anyway but my grandmother's method tells me that it will not rain." She said, "I know how to Tell The Weather, but I will not be telling you how I do it because I do not know you. Why would I tell you anyway? I am just sharing a seat on a crowded bus with you. It is not like I know you."

BUS PASS

We took the X51 from Galway to Limerick. It was the fast bus. It traveled on the new motorway, so the journey was smooth. There was an old man sitting in the front seat up beside the driver. He fell into a deep sleep as soon as the engine started and he slept for the full hour and a half. He woke up as we pulled into Limerick station and he was the first person off the bus. The man wore a short-sleeved tee-shirt and he carried no bag. It did not look like he was going far. The weather was too cold for just a tee-shirt.

We went into the station café for tea and toast while we waited for our connection. The old man came in soon afterwards. He ordered a piece of apple pie. The counter girl poured thick cream over it. He took his pie to a table and he ate it fast. He ate one bite right after another without stopping. He finished the pie and left his plate on the table. The man went up to the counter and ordered a big slice of chocolate layer cake. The counter girl held up the jug of cream and he nodded. She poured a lot of cream onto his cake. There were plenty of empty tables. He could have gone back to the same table where he sat when he ate his pie. Instead he came over to our table and he asked if he could join us. I knew the man wanted to chat. He sat down and he began to eat his cake with the same speed and attention that he had given to his pie eating. He sat down with us even though there were a lot of other empty tables. He looked up from his plate when it was empty. He asked if we lived in Limerick. I said No. I asked if he lived in Limerick. He said No. He said he lived in Galway. He had just come over on the bus for a slice of cake but the pie looked good so he had a piece of pie first and now he was having the cake which is what he came for. The man told us that he was retired and that he used to be a farmer. I asked if he missed the farming and he said No. He said he did not miss the farming, but he did miss the wife. She had been a school teacher but she died two years ago on December the 12th. He said the hardest thing in life was losing your partner. Losing your life partner and living in retirement had a way of making life empty.

The old man said that he enjoys the freedom of his Bus Pass. Every person in the country receives this card at the age of sixty-six. The card gives them freedom to travel on buses and on trains without paying. They can take someone with them if they want. They can take a spouse or a carer or just someone they meet at the bus stop. Two people can travel for free. He enjoys the freedom of his card but he would like it better if the wife could travel along with him. Today he had ridden for an hour and a half to get to Limerick. He ate pie and cake and now he was speaking with us. Soon he would be on the next bus returning to Galway. That would be another hour and a half. He said he could ride the buses all day long. Riding the buses was a way for him to pass the time.

We said goodbye and went out to wait for our connecting bus. I watched the old man come out of the station a few minutes later. He climbed back up and into the X51. He was the first person on the bus. He sat himself in the front seat. We were still waiting for our own bus to arrive when the X51 pulled out and headed back to Galway.

VALLEY BUS

I caught the early bus to Cork. It was dark when I left the house. It was dark and it was cold. By the time I boarded, daylight was breaking. It was no longer dark but it was not yet light. As we motored along the valley road, dawn was illuminating the land. The pink glow of the sun hit the mountains first. Hills and trees and buildings were washed in the warm color that got brighter and brighter even while everything else was not fully lit. I sat on the left side of the bus in order to look out and across at the mountains, enjoying the silent emptiness of the countryside.

As we approached the village, the first house came into view. On the side of the house, someone had painted foot-high capital letters with bright red paint. What was written was: JIMMIE FEENEY RAPED ME. My pleasure in the pastoral and beautiful winter morning was shaken. This village is a small village. There are only 300 people living in it. The population of a village is determined by the number of people living within the speed limit signs.

There are more people in the surrounding countryside, but not a lot more.

I do not know anyone in this village. I do not know who Jimmie Feeney is. Everyone who lives in the village will of course know who Jimmie Feeney is. Everyone will know everything. If they did not know it before, they know it now.

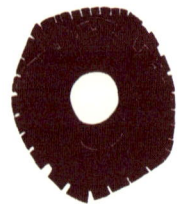

STUCK IN INCHICORE

We were leaving Dublin. A man seated in the middle of the bus was shouting into his phone. No one could read or sleep or think while he was shouting. No one could fail to listen.

"The bitch yeah you heard about it? Yeah she had her head out the window. She loved doing that she did but we went through a skinny bit of the alley backing down and her head hit a pole. Yeah yeah dead right away. Snapped her neck. Not a whimper. Hey who is this anyway? Paddy? Paddy Dorman? Who the hell gave you my number? Who do you think you are ringing me? Paddy Gorman or Paddy Dorman? Oh you're that Paddy. Oh Sorry Paddy I thought you were the other Paddy. You know him yourself. He's a right nuisance that one. We're stuck in Inchicore Paddy. I'm on the bus and we're stuck in Inchicore. We're going down to Tipp to see The Wife's Mother. The Wife she's down there already with The Mother. I'm with The Son. On the bus yeah. She's not well The Mother. Yeah I've got the grapes for The Gift. Yeah Paddy we're on the bus but we're only in Inchicore. We're going nowhere

Paddy. We paid to go to Tipp but we haven't got far. I'm inside on the bus now. Yeah we got on at Busarás. That's where it starts but at this rate we won't get to Tipp till Tuesday. You know yourself Paddy. Once you're on the bus it's like a trap. You can't get off. You've got to go where you paid to go. It was 28 euro for the both of us Paddy. That's what we paid and we're only in Inchicore so in that kind of a way it's an expensive trip but if we ever get to Tipperary we'll feel sure we've had our value for the money we will. We'll feel glad Paddy to be somewhere else."

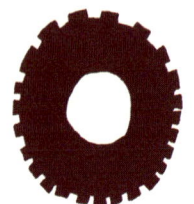

SCENIC ROUTE

There was a great smell on the Number 55 driving out of Limerick. A young man opened a new tin of black boot polish. He had a brush and he had two rags. He spent twenty-five minutes polishing his high-topped black boots. He was listening to something on big earphones the whole time. The young man had two seats to himself so he had plenty of room for his work. He worked quickly and methodically. He rubbed the polish in thoroughly, moving carefully around every area of the entire boot. He then placed that boot on the floor and rubbed polish into the second boot. Leaving the two boots resting on the floor for a few minutes, he looked out the window. He sat absolutely still. If it was music he was listening to on his earphones the music did not show itself in his body. He did not tap or sing or bounce. He sat still and he looked out the window. When he picked up the first boot, he began to rub it slowly with a clean cloth. He did the same with the second boot. Then he left them both resting on the floor again for a few minutes. He picked the first boot up again and buffed it hard and fast with his brush. He brushed and brushed. The boot came up gleaming. This hard and rapid rubbing was repeated several times on both boots. Every single surface and curve was rubbed and rubbed and rubbed. Maybe he was a soldier or maybe he was a Garda trainee. This level of boot cleaning and polishing is not common, especially not on a bus.

Just before arriving in Tipp Town, the man loaded his equipment into a round tin. It was a Christmas tin that had once been full of Cadbury's Heroes. He folded the rags carefully into the tin in such a way that the rest of the things inside would not rattle around. He wrapped the clean boots in a towel and placed them in his large duffel bag. He took off his big earphones. He put them in the bag too. He sat quietly until it was time for him to get off the bus.

The bus could not enter Tipperary Town. There is the county of Tipperary and there is the town of Tipperary. The town of Tipperary is within the county of Tipperary. The town is often spoken of as Tipp Town just to remind people that it is a particular place and not just the huge place that is the whole entire county. There was a protest going on The town center was closed. A march was protesting the lack of jobs in the town. Signs were posted on every building and in the windows of every house and shop: JOBS FOR TIPP TOWN! We could not see the march because the bus was following the signs for diversion. Normally the bus drives straight through the middle of Tipperary Town. Instead we took turn after turn down narrow streets. We drove on streets I had never seen before. We drove on streets that were never meant to have a bus driving down them. The young man with the shiny boots in his duffel bag got off somewhere on the edge of town because the bus could not stop in the usual place. A few other people descended at the same time. The people getting off grumbled about ending up in the incorrect location. One man announced that he was Mighty Aggrieved to be finding himself on the wrong side of town. The young man with the well-polished boots in his bag did not say a word.

The bus continued on its way, taking odd tight turns. We finally left Tipp Town. We were not on the usual route. Everyone on the bus perked up when the diversions continued outside the town. No one knew where we were going. We were on a winding road driving through fields and farms. We were taking the scenic route. It was a lovely bright day to be looking around. There were no more yellow signs redirecting the diverted traffic. There were no signs pointing to any towns or any villages. There were no signs at all. The driver just kept driving and taking a left or a right as the roads got smaller and tighter.

An old woman near the front of the bus shouted up to the driver. She said "Are you going to Galbally then?" He called back to her, "I have never been to Galbally. This is not a bus for Galbally. I am not going to Galbally." She said, "Well, you are going there now because this is the Galbally road." She shouted, "I know this road. I had a cousin in Galbally. I have not been there for two years now. I have never been back to Galbally because my cousin is dead."

The driver cursed and swore. He attempted to make a slow and cumbersome turn in a dangerous spot on a blind corner. The road was too narrow for him to turn around, so he backed up for half a kilometer until we reached the last turn which was a left turn. He took the left and began barreling down that road. He was driving much too fast for such a narrow road.

If the bus met anything at all coming the other way we would have a collision. Lucky for us, no one was on the road. I guess everyone was at the march in Tipp Town. The driver announced out loud that he hoped we were headed in the right direction.

The old woman said, "Oh. Are we not going to Galbally then?" She sounded disappointed. And the whole bus still smelled like boot polish.

HORSE

The woman was the last passenger to board. She was not old but she was not young. She was completely winded as she mounted the steps. She was gasping to catch her breath while she hunted out her money to pay the driver. She had been running down the road in order not to miss the bus. She had been running down the road wearing exactly the wrong kind of shoes for running. An elderly man was sitting in the very front seat. The old man said, "I heard you clattering up behind me. I thought you were a horse."

TWICE

We had a short stop and then the bus left Cashel. After a few minutes, a boy in the back stood up and called to the driver. He shouted, "Hey! You! You left me Mam in Feehan's Bar!"

Cashel had been the first stop since the bus left Dublin. It had been a two hour trip, so several people rushed across the street to use the toilets in Feehan's Bar. The mother had been one of them. The driver himself had smoked a cigarette on the pavement and then he hopped back into the bus. Thinking that everyone was back on board, he closed the door and drove off. When the boy shouted to him, the driver stopped the bus and discussed the situation with the boy, who was about 10. The driver then turned the bus around and drove back into Cashel. The mother was waiting at the bus stop. She did not look upset nor worried. She was just waiting. The door opened to let her on and then the bus turned around again.

Turning a bus around is a slow and cumbersome maneuver. Our bus did it twice. By the time the bus reached its next stop, it was forty-five minutes late.

All the passengers who needed to make connections had already missed their buses.

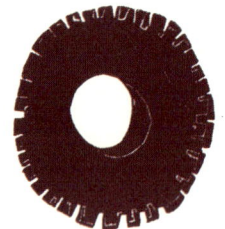

MILKY TEA

A man sat down beside me. I was trapped between him and the window. I always sit near the window if I can because I like to look out at the passing scenery. I always sit by the window and I always hope that the aisle seat will not be occupied. Today a man sat beside me. He was a large man. That is why I felt trapped. There was nowhere to go anyway except where the bus was taking us but having such a large presence so close made me feel claustrophobic.

The man flipped out the little tray table on the seat in front of him. The table pressed into his tummy. He placed two enormous take-away cups of tea on the tray. He was lucky that there was a tray table for his two cups. Some of the new buses have little tray tables and some of the old buses have little tray tables. But not all of any of the buses have the little pull-down tray tables. I would guess that maybe one bus in three has pull-down tables. The man was lucky. I am not sure what he would have done with his two cups of tea without a place to put them.

The man's name was Joe. His friend sat a few seats up ahead and he shouted down to the man calling the name Joe and Joe answered so that is how I knew his name. He chatted away as he settled in. He might have been talking to me or he might have been talking to himself. I could not understand anything he said because he said it all with a strong Cork accent.

Joe sipped his tea quietly for a while and then he began to lick his arms. He had terrible flaking skin on his forearms. He was wearing a short-sleeved shirt because the day was warm. He had dry flaking skin all the way down to his fingers. Where the skin was not flaking or where it had already flaked off, his arms were raw and red. They looked painful. Joe licked his forearms methodically. Up and down. Up and down. It took me a while to realize that before each long careful licking, he was filling his mouth with tea. Joe was using the hot milky tea to soothe his painful arms. In between the licking he stopped and looked across me and out the window at the passing scenery. Sometimes he shouted up the aisle to his friend. Sometimes he just stared straight ahead while he drank tea from one of the big cups.

STAND CLEAR

When the luggage doors on the side of the bus are opening or closing there is a safety announcement to tell everyone who is on the bus and directly outside the bus that this is what is happening. The recorded voice drones *Stand Clear Luggage Doors Operating* again and again. The sentence sounds like each word is separate and even if the words are part of the same sentence they might not be. It is as though there is a full stop after each word. *Stand. Clear. Luggage. Doors. Operating.* The recording is played over and over. The people inside the bus get sucked into the repetition. Very quietly, each person in his or her own seat begins to intone the words. It is a chant. It is like they are singing but they do not realize that they are singing. The bus is full of people chanting together but they do not know it is together. When the recording stops everyone stops chanting and they all go back to whatever they were doing.

NEW LOOK

I took the valley bus from Ardfinnan to Cork this morning. There were very few passengers. It was early so the bus was quiet. We stopped in Clogheen and Ballyporeen and then in Mitchelstown. A lot of people got on in Mitchelstown and the whole bus changed. It was no longer quiet.

Somewhere between Mitchelstown and Fermoy, the young woman who was sitting beside me got a phone call. She spoke respectfully to someone named Michael. She used his name in every sentence. She told him that it was her day off and that she was on her way to Cork. She said she was sorry about his situation and if there was no one else available, of course she would turn around and be there to help him. She told him to get back to her. She spoke in a kind and gentle tone. I thought perhaps she was talking to an elderly person needing a lift to somewhere important like the hospital.

She then made three calls in quick succession to other people. With each person, she discussed Michael and the problem. She was on her way to Cork and it was her day off and she had a hair appointment and then she was meeting some girlfriends for dinner and she had not seen the girls for a long time and she had even made plans to stay the night. Michael phoned again. He said he needed her to be there by 3.30.

She said her hair appointment was at 3.20, so there was no way she could be back by then, but she continued to assure him that she would help in any way she could.

The offers to help and the importance of the hairdressing appointment were at odds with one another. I was not trying to eavesdrop. I kept looking down and trying to read my book but that was difficult. I could not concentrate on my book. I could not help but be involved in the ongoing problem. Her voice got louder and louder each time she discussed the situation with anyone who was not Michael. I did not hear what Michael said as he said it but I heard every word of his conversation as she repeated his words in her other conversations. With Michael himself, she remained calm and quiet. After several more phone calls, I understood that Michael was her boss and whoever she had gotten to cover for her that day had stood him up, so she was needed back at the job.

We arrived in Cork before anything was resolved. I forgot all about her and all about Michael while I did my errands. When I returned to the station for the 3 o'clock bus to take me back to Ardfinnan, I found myself looking around for the young woman among the people who were already in line waiting to board. I wondered if she was heading back to help Michael or if she was on her way to the hairdressers by now. I never had a proper look at her face. I did not think I would recognize her but I thought I might recognize her bright blue trousers.

As for her hair, she was planning on getting a completely New Look so there was no chance of me recognizing her by her hair.

She had announced several times to the people on the phone who were not Michael that she had found the New Look in a magazine at the dentist's office and she had torn the page out to show it to the hairdresser. She had the page in her bag. She patted her bag each time she mentioned the New Look. A lot of the same people who had been on the bus in the morning were on the return bus with me, but she was not among them.

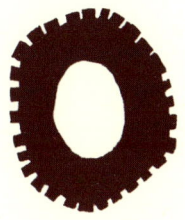

NO LUCK

We were surprised that the bus from Dublin airport was such an old bus. It was a town bus. It was a double-decker and not the usual sort of bus to drive long distances. The X8 buses are normally high and modern and they have large automatic doors on one side to slide luggage into. This bus was so low to the ground that everyone had to drag their bags and cases into the bus with them. We each had to try to find a place for our stuff in between seats. Since we were beginning our journey from the airport, every single person had luggage to store. No one was boarding the bus empty-handed. As we entered the bus, the driver advised us not to go upstairs. He said that we could go up there if we wanted but he recommended that we not go upstairs. He said it was roasting hot up there. He told each person who boarded that he had No Knowledge of how to turn off the heat. This was not his usual bus. He said this was not his usual route. He said there was No Luck in this bus. He did not know what desperate thing he had done in this lifetime or the last to be given this terrible bus for the day.

A young man from the Indian subcontinent climbed onto the bus behind us. He told the driver in very careful English that he wanted to go to Cork. The driver told the Indian lad that he might enjoy the heat upstairs. He said, "But you will be the only one." He said, "Not one other person will like it." He told the Indian lad that no matter where he chose to sit for the journey, he himself would wake him up in Cork. He said that it would be at least four hours until the bus reached Cork but he reassured the Indian lad again and again by saying, "No Worries. I will wake you up if you are asleep when we get there."

The bus was old and shaky. As soon as we set off, it began to rain. The downstairs of the bus was freezing cold. The bus was not made for motorway speed. We could not go as fast as the bus was scheduled to go. We just puttered along. The windscreen wipers were squeaky and loud. It was dark. There was nothing to be seen outside the bus. Except for an occasional lit window in the distance, there were no lights anywhere in the countryside. Since the bus was not made to function as a long-distance bus we had no reading lights. We sat in the dark and we looked out into the dark.

Cashel was the first stop out of Dublin. It had already been three hours. By the time we got there, we were well late. A young woman told the driver she was desperate for the loo. Our bus was too old to have a toilet on board. The driver told her to run across the road to Feehan's Bar. She left her belongings on the bus. He promised that we would wait for her. The driver sang us a song while we waited. He had a fine voice. He stood at the front of the bus and he sang with a strong Cork accent. It was not a song that I recognized. We all applauded politely when he finished. He did not sing a second song. He sat back in his driving seat and waited for the woman. The woman was taking a long time but no one said anything about that. It would not have been polite. The bus was already late. Everyone on the bus was already late for wherever they were going. Being later was not going to matter much.

Water was running down the aisle. It was just a small trickle of water. I thought it was rain water. I assumed the bus had a leak. It was not rain water.

The man behind me was going through his bag of groceries trying to find out what was leaking. He announced each item as he pulled it out of the bag. He announced each item and he enunciated loudly and carefully. He decided it must be the bottle of water at the very bottom of the bag. He assured everyone who was in listening distance that he usually packs carefully so that nothing leaks.

When the woman finally returned from the loo, she looked dreadful. She went upstairs into the heat. We set off again. The Indian lad had not gone upstairs to the heat. He was sitting beside the man with the leaking bag. He explained clearly and slowly to the man that he needed to get off in the town of Fermoy which was in the county of Cork. He did not need to go all the way to the city of Cork. The man with the leaking bag explained that after Cahir and after Mitchelstown, the very next stop would be Fermoy. It would be the third stop. A woman across the aisle leaned over. She said that she herself was getting off at Fermoy so she said she would alert the man from India as to exactly when he needed to descend from the bus. She said he could just follow her. The driver heard all of this and he shouted down the aisle that he would be calling out Good and Noisy-Like when the bus reached Fermoy.

We got off in Cahir. With so much help from the driver and the other passengers, I have no doubt that the Indian lad got off in Fermoy without any problem. Everyone was eager to make him feel welcome because they knew that he was far from his home.

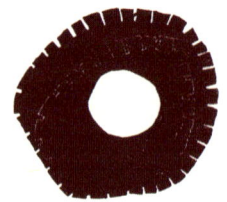

A NEVER-MARRIED

Sibby told me about her friend Carmel who came to live in the village a few years ago. Carmel was on the public housing and they had offered her a newly built apartment over the hardware shop. She did not know anyone at all in the village but she took the flat because she liked the idea of living in a brand new place with brand new appliances. She loved the idea of a brand new toilet. She relished the idea of living in a place that no one else had ever lived in.

Carmel and Sibby met while riding the Ring-A-Link bus into town. The Ring-A-Link is just that. In order to get a lift, you ring a number and tell them the time that you hope or need to be in town the next day. They write your name down and then they ring back to tell you what time they will pick you up. They ring to tell you your place in the link. Sometimes you get picked up early and you go fairly straight into town. Other times you get picked up and you ride along in the bus as it meanders through the countryside stopping in villages, town lands or at the end of someone's drive. It can take as long as one hour to get to town. Directly, by car, it is a 15 minute drive from Sibby's house to the town, but that is when her son drives her, which he rarely does.

Everyone on the Ring-A-Link gets to know one another pretty quickly. It is not a large bus. There are only 20 passengers on any one trip. The ten seats hold two passengers each. By the time the bus gets to town, the bus is full and everyone knows a lot about each other. They all know what everyone else is planning to do in the town. And everyone on the bus already knows where most of the other passengers live because they see exactly where the driver picks them up and drops them off. There is not a lot of privacy on the Ring-A-Link.

The passengers are instructed to meet in front of Eason's at the end of the day for the return journey. If the driver is one of the agreeable drivers he might be willing to stop to pick someone up at the bottom of the hill near the hospital or even in front of the residential home for the elderly.

Sibby tells me that one of the drivers is nice but the other one is too crabby to accommodate anyone at all.

Sibby herself goes to town every other day to visit her husband who is in a care home. She knows everyone who rides the Ring-A Link.

Carmel rides the Ring-a-Link most days without actually needing to go anywhere. She is riding the bus because she is hoping to meet a man. Everywhere she goes and everything she does is about trying to meet a man. She does not mind if the man is A Widower or A Never-Married. Sibby says that Carmel would rather not find a man who is still living with his mother, but she is not too fussy.

Some days Carmel goes to the Garden Centre for her dinner. She says a lot of single men, as well as many priests, go there because the restaurant does a good roast with plenty of vegetables and potatoes at midday. Carmel has told Sibby that if these men had someone cooking for them at home they would not need to be coming out for a big cooked dinner in the middle of the day. Carmel has established many methods for identifying and locating unmarried men. The Garden Centre is one way but riding the buses is her preferred way. She likes the amount of time allotted to talk with someone. She says that she can ask as many questions as she wants to ask and the man is not able to escape, because he is on the bus.

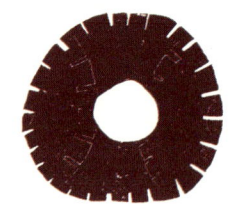

RAIN

I am on the bus. We are traveling through lashing rain. It is just getting dark. There is a television screen above the windscreen in the bus. The TV screen shows the road ahead of us. For those of us sitting close to the front, we can see both the road ahead and the movie of the road ahead that shows on the screen. Passengers in the back of the bus can only see the movie version of our journey through the rain. There are huge windscreen wipers on the front of the bus. The camera is somehow angled so that we see windscreen wipers on the TV screen too. The two different sets of wipers, large and small, are both visible and they move in unison.

Red digital dots above the screen tell the time. Minute by minute we can watch the movie of our journey. We can see the road and we can see the movie. We see every minute as it passes in digital time.

There is a lot of water on the road. The water reflects the headlights of other vehicles. When we pass through a town there is an eerie blue and yellow glow over everything in the TV version of that town. A red car looks pink. Everything in the movie of our trip looks garish and unreal. The rain in the movie is more relentless than the rain out the windows.

CONGEALED MILK

It did not take long for everyone on the bus to learn that the man was a taxi driver in Dublin. He had been a taxi driver in Dublin for a long time. We discovered that he had been a taxi driver because he was speaking on his mobile telephone. The taxi driver had a loud voice. His voice carried from one end of the bus to the other. We were all in on his side of the conversation.

We could not hear what was being said on the other end of the phone. We only had his half of the conversation. We did not really need to hear the other speaker. We did not need to hear any of it.

We were already hearing much more than we wanted to hear.

The someone on the other end of the telephone was maybe considering becoming a taxi driver himself. Or maybe he was already a taxi driver. Maybe he was trying to convince the man to return to driving a taxi at night. Our taxi driver on the bus said that he only drove days now. He said he had his reasons.

"If they vomit, that is it for the night. You just have to give up and go home."

"If I were ever to go back to driving nights, I would want to get leather seats."

"It's when they are trying to hold it in, that's the problem."

"Yeah, one night I saw one of the new drivers at the car wash. He had not been on the job for long. Hosing out the whole inside of the car, he was, and crying all the while."

"The smell. Yeah. The smell is like congealed milk. It never goes away."

PLACES NAMED

There is now a service called the AirCoach which goes back and forth between Cork and Dublin Airport. It only makes a few stops. Each place where the AirCoach stops is well marked with a bright orange sign. The sign now tells us the name of the place where we have always been stopping on the regular bus but until now we did not know the name of the place. It was always just The Bus Stop, which was outside a particular bar or a shop in a particular town or village, and there is never more than one stop of the bus per place.

When the Bus Éireann stopped today in Mitchelstown I noticed that the new AirCoach sign announced it as Mitchelstown New Square. I never knew that the big square was called New Square. I did not need to know the name of the square because I never get on or off the bus in Mitchelstown, and anyway there is only the one stop in town.

Thursday is market day in Mitchelstown. The square which I now know to call New Square was busy. It was full of stalls and people. A crowd of people was waiting to board our bus. This is not normal. There were at least thirty people bunching up together to get on. Everyone who was already on the bus got excited. They discussed amongst themselves that this was the most people they had ever seen boarding the bus in Mitchelstown. Everyone worried that this many passengers might not all be able to fit onto our bus. The bus was noisy with excited anticipation. The driver worried out loud that it was taking too long to get them loaded. Some people did not have the right money and others had awkward bundles or babies and prams. The driver despaired with a big mournful voice because he knew he would be late for his scheduled arrival in Cork.

A BAG OF GUNS

She had been waiting for her niece who had left her bags behind at The McDonald's Restaurant. The niece forgot her bags at The McDonald's and she had had to run back and now Betty was on the bus with lots of shopping bags and the niece was nowhere to be seen. She said "I am older than her but I never forget anything. I look behind me when I stand up. She is just young. Well, she will be 22 next month so she is not that young. I am waiting for the niece because almost all these bags are hers. I don't want to walk all the way up the hill in Fermoy with all this, now do I?"

The bus was already late leaving the station. The driver came down the aisle and counted the empty seats. He returned to the front and he spoke to some people waiting outside. He said he only had two seats left. We heard the discussion between the driver and the hopeful passengers. One lad said it was fine by him as he could sit on the lap of The Big Fellow. The driver said okay and three boys got on. As promised, the smallest lad sat on the lap of the biggest one. A few minutes later the driver let another girl on because she said her aunt was already on board and she said the aunt had all the shopping with her and the aunt would not be able for carrying it all the way up the hill in Fermoy by herself if the young one waited for the next bus. The driver let her on and she sat on the floor by the toilet. She was Betty's niece.

Her name was Betty but that was not her given name. Her name was not Elizabeth. Her name was Gwendolyn. Betty came out of Gwendolyn but she did not know why and no one in her family knew why. She explained that she had always been Betty.

She spoke loudly and since I was in the next seat across the aisle, I could not do anything but listen. I knew I would not be able to read nor to sleep. Her voice took over everything in range. The person in the seat beside her was a complete captive.

"That's a fine chemist and they are reasonable too. They are open till 8 o'clock." As we leave the town, Betty announces everything she knows about anything the bus passes at the moment of passing.

She points out the Polish shop and she says, "They need to have their own shops because they prefer to eat their own food."

Once on the highway there is less to talk about because there are only fields to be seen out the windows. Betty continues talking anyway. The one thing she does not do is stop talking. She talks about whatever comes into her head.

"Last week I wanted to go to Cork but I missed the bus because they had changed the times and I did not know about it. It was on the paper and it was on the radio but I do not read the paper and I do not own a radio so I got it wrong but my friend has a radio, so now she tells me if there is anything that I need to know."

"We are not worried about those floods over in England. We have enough water of our own to worry about. We have more water than we can be going on with. Who cares if they drown over there. We take care of our own."

"I was on a shopping trip to Penneys. I had to get down for the sales. I know they say it is going to rain again tomorrow, but I don't care, do I? I'll be at home and I'll be dry. Today I had to go to the sales. You are holding one of my niece's big full-up shopping bags on your knee which is good of you. It is very good of you. What would I have done with all these bags if you had not offered to hold one on your knee?"

"If you live in Mitchelstown and I live in Fermoy we are sure to know some of the same people. There are people going back and forth between those two towns all the time. Some get married to people out of town and some just move for the work. It is good to mix things up. It's like cats on a farm. You need to bring in fresh blood otherwise the cats start behaving stupid because the genes get repeated and then they get stepped on by the cows. You must know Kitty and Liam. Let me tell you where they live. When I first met Liam he thought Tony and I were married. Tony was my brother. We had a laugh on that. Tony died in Oh Five of The Parkinson. It wasn't The Cancer. Every second person has The Cancer now. It is out of control. The government needs to do something about it. He was pale enough by the time he died."

She shouted down to her niece on the floor in the center of the bus near the toilet that they would be getting off soon. She turned back to her seatmate and said, "I saw a bag of guns being put in with the luggage under the bus. I saw it when I was waiting on line. They were made of wood. Some were painted but some of them weren't painted yet. I was not scared by seeing the guns but I was surprised."

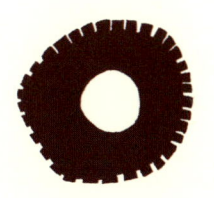

GET THE SHEEP

The man in the seat behind me was urging the woman to photograph the sheep from the bus window. She had the window seat and he was on the aisle. She had a fancy camera. He had the enthusiasm. He was directing her. She did not say a word. There were two or three sheep in a far field and then there were a few more in another field close to a stone wall. It was not a flock of sheep. It was just a few stragglers off and away from a larger group. The first few had bright orange paint on them. He was excited about both clumps of sheep. He repeated: "Get the Sheep. Get the Sheep. Get the Sheep."

When the bus had passed the sheep and there were no more sheep to be seen, he continued to direct the woman with occasional suggestions or orders. There was a loud click as each photograph was taken. The man turned and spoke with the couple across the aisle. They were looking out their own side of the bus and taking their own photographs. They were more than a little put out when he mentioned the sheep. They had seen no sheep.

When the bus rolled down the hill into Cahir the man directed the woman: "Get the weir. Get the river. Get the geese. Get the geese." The woman snapped and snapped. The man made happy moaning sounds. He was well pleased. The couple on the other side of the bus were also rapidly making photographs. They had the castle on their side of the bus. The man and woman behind me saw the river and the weir and the steeple of the small John Nash church in the curve of the river, but they missed the castle. The people on the far side of the bus missed the view downriver. They had the castle but not the river. They were friends who were traveling together, but not together.

POOR MISFORTUNATES

A young man boarded the bus along with us at the airport. He was carrying a large bouquet of flowers. It was a blousy extravagant bouquet in white cellophane paper. The paper was like an enormous upside-down show-off skirt. I do not know where he bought such a bouquet. I do not think there are flowers for sale anywhere at the airport. I think this man must have bought the bouquet somewhere else. He must have arrived at the airport with the flowers but it was not to give the flowers to someone just off a plane from somewhere because he had no one with him. He did not have a suitcase. He just had the flowers. Now he was boarding our bus and taking the flowers somewhere else. The entire bus smelled of his bouquet. It was a bit much. There were enormous lilies and something else with a strong smell. The man wedged his bouquet high up into a crack between the two seats in front of him so he could enjoy the journey and have his hands free while the flowers were safe from any crushing and damage.

Before leaving Dublin, we made a stop at Busarás, the central bus station. Two people heavily laden with plastic carrier bags stuffed full of things got on the bus. The people looked very poor and very unhappy. A terrible smell arrived with them. Suddenly the flower fumes that had seemed overwhelming during the journey from the airport to the station seemed not so bad. There would be at least two hours between leaving the Busarás and our first stop. No one would be able to get off the bus. This was a daunting prospect. I wondered if I would be able to stand it. An older woman leaned across the aisle towards me and she sort of cooed: "Oh the Poor Poor Misfortunates." She sighed heavily and went back to her book.

Traffic was bad and the bus was slow. The two hour journey took three hours. I was sitting near the front of the bus. The bouquet was propped up in its position of safety in the center of the bus. The Poor Misfortunates sat all the way in the back of the bus. I suppose I was lucky in a way. From where I sat, the smells canceled each other out and I was far enough away to able to forget about them, at least for some of the time.

MEET ME

The lady in front of me got out her phone and rang to tell someone that we were just leaving Cashel and that she would arrive in Mitchelstown in three quarters of an hour.

She said, "I'll be at the bus stop."

She said, "I will walk up to the Tesco."

Again, she said, "I will walk up to the Tesco." She said, "Meet me at the Tesco."

She said, "You go to Tesco and I'll go to Tesco."

She said, "We'll meet at the Tesco."

Maybe she was talking to someone who was hard of hearing. Making this plan seemed very difficult. It was still being discussed when I got off the bus in Cahir. I was exhausted by the repetition.

THE BLACK CLOTHES

The X8 was travelling up from Cork. Eventually it would arrive in Dublin. The woman was speaking on the phone. Sometimes she was weeping.

Nobody cares anymore if their conversation is overheard. It does not matter if you are listening to one side of a phone conversation or if you are listening to two people talking to one another. Words are not private.

This woman was obsessed by her Black Clothes. The Black Clothes had been left in a suitcase. The suitcase was left on the plane. There had been so many things to gather together and pack and bring home that one suitcase had been left behind and the airline had not been able to locate it. Or the airline had not been able to locate it yet. Maybe they would locate it in the near future but the woman had little faith in this possibility. She was praying and all of her family were praying and maybe God Willing the suitcase would reappear. The Black Clothes are what really mattered to her. She needed the Black Clothes that she had worn on the day.

The son had died in Australia or maybe it was New Zealand. It was somewhere far away and the son's death had been sudden and unexpected. He was a young man after all. She and the husband had gone out to collect the body and to do everything that had to be done. There had been a lot to do. They had a Mass for the son before they left wherever they were. That was just a ceremony for his brief life out there. They brought the body home for the proper burial.

The mother had the very last pack of cigarettes that the son bought before he died. She had them with her in her handbag. The last pack had been in his apartment with his things. There were six cigarettes left. He had died with six remaining cigarettes. He was probably saving the six for the morning to smoke with his tea. Six cigarettes was enough for the siblings and the father and herself to each have one. She planned that she would share them out and they would all smoke them after the burial. Except for her. She was going to save hers. She would never smoke it. It was the last cigarette her son had ever bought. She would never smoke it. She would save it.

She had worn the Black Clothes on the day for the far-away Mass. Now she was needing those same Black Clothes for the burial. She repeated again and again that she was needing the Black Clothes that she wore on the day. They could not be replaced by any other black garments. She had the cigarettes but the Black Clothes were in the suitcase. The suitcase was nowhere to be found.

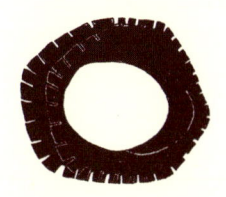

IMELDA

We are on the way to Dublin. As the bus enters a town somewhere along the route, a red Ford Fiesta passes at great speed. The bus swerves. The brakes squeal. Everyone shrieks or moans. The extremely quiet bus is suddenly in chaos. At the first stoplight, the Ford Fiesta is right in front of us. A group of older ladies in the first seats of the bus read out the license plate number. These five ladies all call out the number separately and together. They repeat it several times. A man with a mobile phone rings the Garda to report the dangerous driver. He announces to everyone in a loud voice that he is going to report the driver and then he announces again that he has just reported the driver. Every single person on the bus is watching every move of the red car. Every single one of us feels personally threatened by the wild driving. The bus follows the dangerous driver right through the town and then the car races off passing more vehicles at speed. Once the red car is out of sight, there is still a feeling of excitement and panic in the bus. The Near Disaster experience has joined everyone in a sort of kinship.

There are a lot of sparkly dresses on the bus. Most of the women on board, including the five up in the front, are on their way to a performance of Imelda May in Dublin. That explains why they are all dressed up. As a result of all of the chatter and the near death crash, many of the women on board have recognized each other to all be heading to the same event. If the bus had crashed, they agree that the absence of our busload would have made a sizable dent in Imelda's audience. All the women agree how grand it is to have survived. They are all looking forward to the performance. Every one of them speaks of Imelda by her first name. The use of the first name assumes a level of closeness and intimacy. The use of the first name makes Imelda into family. They all adore Imelda May. Everyone agrees how dreadful it would have been if they had missed the concert altogether. It would have been terrible to have disappointed Imelda.

TICK TIES

The two lads were sitting behind me on the bus. We were going to Cork and they were going to Cork too. One of them spoke of TICK TIES. He said it once and then he said it again. I had not been listening to their conversation but these two words were repeated again and again. I could not understand the words so I had to listen in order to put them into context. It was a bit like hearing a few words that I do understand in the midst of a sentence in a foreign language. The familiar words move the rest of the conversation into an idea of public business. I think this was the same kind of situation.

Some people do it and some people do not do it. It does not seem to be a spoken quirk from one specific county. Or I cannot tell if it is something that belongs to a particular place. I just hear it sometimes and sometimes I do not hear it. I think it is more like a kind of a lisp or speech defect. Or maybe it is a pronunciation thing carried over from the Irish language. It is the pronouncing of a T instead of a TH, usually at the beginning of a word. When a person says T instead of TH, the entire meaning of the word they are saying can be different.

Eventually I understood that TICK TIES were actually THICK THIGHS. It was THICK THIGHS with the T sound replacing the TH sound. The lad doing most of the talking was discussing his three years in Australia. The second lad was on his way to Australia so the first one was telling him what to expect and what problems might be encountered. Apparently a major issue is that the legs of Irish men are not like the legs of Australian men. If you are the kind of lad with Thick Thighs, the difference in the leg shape makes the simple purchase of a new pair of jeans into a real and pressing problem. And these two lads were both the kind of lads with Thick Thighs. Many Irish lads have Thick Thighs. The Australians do not have the same kind of leg shape so their blue jeans are made to fit their body type. Australian jeans are not comfortable for an Irish lad's legs. In fact they are impossible for the majority of Irish lads' legs. And besides, the Australian jeans are too long. Even the shortest leg length is too long.

The first fellow had located a website that sold blue jeans for the Irish expatriate community. The jeans were cut wider in the thighs and shorter in the leg and they were just as good off the internet as what you could buy right here at home. It was easier to use the website than it was to ask your mother to go and shop for you and post you a pair of jeans. The instructing lad ended this portion of the conversation by saying, "After all, she is your Mam. She would only be after believing that you cannot dress yourself without her help."

A GET-OFF-THE-BUS-WITH-NO-THANK-YOU PERSON

It is an insult. To describe someone as A Get-Off-the-Bus-With-No-Thank-You Person is harsh criticism. It is different for passengers on the city buses. But on any bus journey from the countryside into a town, or from the town into the country or from village to village, it is not an option to leave a bus without saying thank you to the driver. Someone who can do that is not a good person. Someone who can do that says more bad about themselves than any fine thing that they might do for the rest of the day.

Erica Van Horn is an artist and writer. Born in New Hampshire in 1954, she has lived in Europe since the early eighties: France, Britain, and now rural Ireland, where she works together with the poet and artist Simon Cutts on the projects of Coracle. Publications include *Black Dog White Bark*, with Louis Asekoff (Visual Studies Workshop), *Seven Lady Saintes* (Women's Studio Workshop), *Living Locally* (Uniformbooks), *Too Raucous For A Chorus* (Coracle), which was translated and published as *Nous avons de pluie assez eu* (Héros Limite), as well as a forthcoming pamphlet in their series L'Ours Blanc. Also forthcoming is *Fossil* (A Published Event). Her work has appeared in *Whitewalls*, *Tether*, *The Recorder: American Irish Historical Society*, and *Damn the Caesars*, among other publications.

By Bus

Copyright © Erica Van Horn, 2021

ISBN 978-1-946433-73-2

First Edition, First Printing, 2021

Ugly Duckling Presse
The Old American Can Factory
232 Third Street #E-303
Brooklyn, NY 11215

www.uglyducklingpresse.org

Distributed in the USA by SPD/Small Press Distribution

Distributed in the UK by Inpress Books

Design and typesetting by Michael Newton & Don't Look Now!

The type is Sabon and OCR A Std

Books printed offset and bound at McNaughton & Gunn

Covers printed letterpress at Ugly Duckling Presse

The publication of this book was made possible, in part, by the New York State Council on the Arts with the support of Governor Andrew M. Cuomo and the New York State Legislature. This project is supported by the Robert Rauschenberg Foundation.